A Common Economic System Architecture

Freedom and Justice by Design
Re-designing Capitalism

Robert Wootton

Copyright © 2014 by Robert Wootton.

All rights reserved.

This book describes a possible global economic system that makes it in the economic self interest for business owners, managers and shareholders to create full time jobs, reduce overtime working to a minimum and to be financially/morally responsible in their business affairs. To reduce the demand by governments for more and more taxes and to encourage and enable their citizens to be self reliant.

I dedicate this book to the memory of Stafford Beer.

THESIS

SECOND STATEMENT

We shall not succeed

in reforming our concept of organization

or in creating new institutions that actually work

simply by hard work -- or even hard thought

We need to invoke SCIENCE – defined as

The organized body of human knowledge

about the world and its workings.

Science offers the means

- To measure and manipulate complexity

    through mathematics

- to design complex systems

    through general systems theory

- to devise viable organizations

    through cybernetics

- to work *effectively* with people

    through behavioral science

- to apply all this to practical affairs

    through operational research

In using these essentially interdisciplinary capabilities

science is free to draw on its depository of knowledge

of physical, biological and social systems.

The knowledge and the skills exist

But are wasted – frivolled away.

Society proceeds instead by *consensus*

That lowest common denominator of alternative democracies

which buys protection against

megalomaniacs, fascists, charlatans and lunatics

and which also protects us from

novelty, unique ability, change and leadership.

The consensus simplifies, distorts and makes trivial

The real problems of complexification

which are inherently too difficult

for *all* to understand.

Platform for Change, page 49, Stafford Beer 1975 ISBN 0 471 06189 1

The work of Stafford Beer has been a big influence on my life ever since I read "Designing Freedom" in 1975, followed by "Platform for Change", "Decision and Control" and the second edition of "Brain of the Firm". This has an appendix about the attempt to give the electorate of Chile direct control or influence on ministerial decision making by using the computers and technology that was available at the time. Personal Computers were just coming into the consumer market place. Hard drive capacity was measured in kilobytes!

But it was a statement Beer wrote in one of his books, I think it was "Brain of the Firm" that has inspired me to write this book. The statement was something like this. "Technology can now do anything that can be (precisely?) specified. Therefore you do not have to be an expert or a technocrat to say what can or cannot be done. It is time for the (ordinary?) people to start specifying." I am that ordinary person who has started specifying. I call upon the academic and professional communities and groups such as the Metaphorum.org group, Scio.org and Systems Thinking World to enable the construction of a viable socio-economic system.

Why have I designed this economic system? First, I want to make poverty history. Secondly, to create the conditions for the citizens of the world to be self reliant, healthy, wealthy and highly educated. Thirdly, to minimize government and its associated bureaucracy and red tape. To set the people, and businesses, free from the burden of ever increasing regulation; and exhortations made by government funded organizations telling its citizens how to live their lives.

This book describes the components of a national economy, their internal structure and the protocols and rules governing the relationship amongst them. The integrated structure of the economic system will enable real time monitoring of the economy by government ministers. And because of the recursive nature of a viable economic system, the directors of individual firms will be enabled to monitor the state of their own businesses in real time.

TABLE OF CONTENTS

Preface	1
Introduction	3
Part One The Meta System of the EU	5
Chapter 1 The Components of the Common System Architecture	6
Chapter 2 The Banking System of the EU	7
Chapter 3 The Business Components of the EU	9
Chapter 4 The Contract Law of the EU	10
Part Two The System in Focus, the UK Political Economy	11
Chapter 5 The Banking System of the UK	12
Appendix to Chapter 5	15
Chapter 6 The Taxation Regulations for the Banking and Financial Sector	17
Chapter 7 The Business Components of the UK	19
Appendix to Chapter 7	21
Chapter 8 The Taxation Regulations for the Utilities and Business Components	22
Chapter 9 The Benefit System of the UK	24
Chapter 10 The Contract Law of the UK	27
Appendix The Purpose and Problems of the Common Economic System Architecture	29
Acknowledgements	31

Preface

This book is primarily for the people, politicians and civil servants of the EU and the UK. The concepts and design of this new economic operating system is open source and can...and must be tested by the economic and political think tanks in the UK and the EU.

The first reason why this book is being written is because the social-economic systems that have developed over the centuries are based on centuries old technology; the technology of the quill pen and the printing press. This has elsewhere been called quill pen technology. This is the source of the problem of the current global and Euro-zone and UK economic crises. Although we have the advanced technology of computers, transistors and the developing memsistors, politicians, civil servants and people generally, think in terms of a quill pen technology. In other words, computers are used as electronic filing cabinets in which to store information, usually about people. This is a gross misuse of technology. The original name for a computer is an analytical engine or a calculating machine. They should be used as such.

The second reason is that since the Second World War, a new science has arisen; the science of cybernetics. The original definition of cybernetics by Norbert Weiner is the science of communication and control in the animal and the machine. I understand this to mean that the laws of communication, (like the laws of gravity in the physical world), hold true whether the communication, by whatever means, within an organism, (the human body) or an organization, (the institution of government) or between and amongst organizations, (departments of government).

Government departments and institutions have multiplied over time without regard for these laws of communication, which is why that no government department is fit for purpose.

What is described and advocated in this e-book is an integrated economic operating system that allows real time monitoring of the economy at different levels of recursion, national, regional (EU) and global for those economies governments and citizens that choose to use the system.

In effect what I am advocating is to dual-boot national economies with the integrated real-time economic operating system to run alongside the existing bureaucratic operating system. In much the same way as a computer can be dual booted with two operating systems, e.g. Windows XP and Windows 7 or a Linux based operating system. Which system is used is decided by the user. In the case of the new economic system, the users are the citizens, employees, employers and business people.

The job of government is to implement the components of the Common Economic System Architecture and the protocols within and amongst them in law. **Since this system does not yet exist, it follows that the system will have no effect on any citizen unless and until they voluntarily choose to use the system.**

I call upon the European Parliament to legislate to bring the Common Economic System Architecture into existence and for the president of the European Central Bank and the ECB to take the lead in establishing the new Banking System across the EU.

Introduction.

The reason for this book being written is that no-one else seems to be able to see that it is the structure of our governmental institutions and the existing relationships between and amongst them actually create the social and economic crises that abound today.

This work is an attempt to create a real time economic regulatory operating system for the European Union that will enable the European Commission and the European Central Bank to monitor the EU G.D.P. and the G.D.P. of member states in real time, i.e. week by week or month by month. And for the governments of the member states to monitor their own G.D.P. and devise policies to bring about their politically desired outcomes.

At present, the member states of the EU are completely different from each other in terms of language, cultural patterns of value, social patterns of value, traditional patterns of value and demographics. What they all have in common is a bureaucratic regulatory operating system of government that has been built up piecemeal over the centuries. It is for this reason that the policy initiatives of all the governments do not work or have unintended and undesirable consequences or side effects. In other words, governmental regulation does not work; it is not fit for purpose.

It is not by accident that I have used the phrase bureaucratic regulatory operating system. Just as a computer can be dual-booted with two completely different operating systems, I am advocating that the European Parliament legislate to bring into existence a Common Economic System Architecture that will enable real time monitoring of the economy and enable a real time operating system that will reduce bureaucracy, support businesses, and increase the wealth of every EU citizen.

It will be necessary for the European Parliament to act adventurously and experimentally to bring this alternative operating system into existence. It may allay the fears of MEPs to say that to do this, it will not affect the lives of any EU citizen at all! It will only affect people if they choose to use and work under the new system. So why should people choose to work under the new system? The first reason is that it will be in their own self-interest to do so because it (the system) will enable people to end exploitation, make poverty history, minimize government red tape, guarantee the cash flow of businesses, increase the self reliance of citizens and enable their self actualization, re Maslow's Hierarchy of Needs.

The book is divided into two parts. The first part describes a generic (for the EU as a whole) Common Economic System Architecture and the Contract Law that governs the relationship amongst them. The second part is the System in Focus. This covers the detailed fine tuning of the internal connections within and amongst the system components of the social-economic system of the UK. I have chosen the UK system because I am a UK citizen with in depth experience of working and living under the taxation and benefit system in the lowest percentile of the UK income distribution.

I have studied cybernetics and systems thinking intermittently, since the mid 1970's. The system described is designed to enable the cybernetic laws that govern the behavior of systems to be implemented. These include the Law of Requisite Variety, variety attenuation and amplification and to enable continuous algedonic monitoring of systemic outputs. If you have never heard of these terms, see VSM, the Viable System Model, in Wikipedia.

It will be evident from this book that I am a lay person; not an expert. The design is based on the assumption that some of the system drivers are the desire to minimize the burden of taxation and the requirements of a bureaucratic system of control and regulation; and the desire of the citizen to have control over their own lives and living conditions.

To use systems terminology, there is a need to attenuate government bureaucracy and to amplify the power of the citizen. For any system to be viable, there must be an upper and lower limit to the crucial variables that pertain to the system that is observed.

N.B. The term "EU" can be replaced by the reader as "the US Federal Government" or the "Indian Government" or the Canadian Government. The term "UK" can be replaced by the "State Government" or the "Provincial Government" depending upon the citizenship of the reader.

Part One. The Meta System of the E.U.

What constitutes the economic Meta system of the E.U. are the Banking System, the different types of business organization and the contractual law that governs the relationships between and amongst them. These components and their relationships form the Common Economic System Architecture that can be adopted by any or all member states. Of course there is no reason why any other nation state cannot adopt this system architecture. This includes the Middle Eastern countries, the USA, India, China, Japan, etc., etc.

What it does not specify is the taxation levels and contractual arrangements and penalties except as guideline figures and percentages. However, there are taxation and wage levels and the criteria for setting them; and the contractual arrangements and enforcement that are specified are in Part Two. This is for the System in Focus, the UK political economy.

To enable the real time monitoring of the national economies of the member states and the economy of the EU as a whole, it is a necessary that a code number that is given to each wage and salary payment made into each citizen's bank account. This number must identify a) the job, b) the industry sector and c) the geographical location (not the address) of the recipient. And perhaps, the geographical location of the workplace in which the recipient earned the wage or salary. This would enable the calculation of commuting miles if this is deemed necessary. However, different member states would most probably use different code numbers for the same job and industry sector. This would make it difficult for the EU to collate the economic information that would enable the real time monitoring of the EU economy. Either the EU must impose a standard coding system across the whole Common Economic System Architecture in legislation. Or someone with the expertise of Tim Berners-Lee needs to devise protocols that will enable the different coding systems of the member states to be collated. I most certainly do not have that expertise.

Chapter 1. The Components of the System Architecture.

These include three basic types of business organization; the equitable Public Limited Company, the "eqPLC", the Social Enterprise Company, the sePLC and the Community Interest Company, the ciPLC and two types of self employment; the Public sole trader and the private sole trader; and the Banking system and a new type of contract; the Mutually Agreed Contract Terms contract. The relationships within and amongst the business and banking components and the employees and customers are specified.

A government regulates its country by means of taxation, benefits and by imposing laws and penalties. However, government also regulates its citizens by the way their departments carry out their statutory duties.

In Part Two, I give an explanation of how the operation of the taxation and benefit system in the UK creates the social problems the country faces. These relationships are specified with regard to the economic laws of Supply and Demand, Adam Smith's observation that it is out of self interest that goods and services are provided, not altruism. But the invisible hand of capitalism will become the visible hand of self interest with this system. However, since the system is based on the principles Fairness and Freedom, I do not think that this transparency of economic activity will or should be a reason for a state or entrepreneurs not to adopt the system. Indeed, a working title of this book is Freedom and Fairness by Design.

With regard to the EU, the entitlement to benefits for citizens living in member states other than their home country will be considered here.

When an EU citizen moves to another member state and legitimately claims a benefit, then the total benefits paid by that state is deducted from that state's EU contribution and that amount is added to the EU contribution that is payable by the benefit recipients' home state.

However, this is a complex matter that requires further analysis and another book.

Chapter 2. The Banking System of the EU.

.

The banking system for the EU is based on rules for protecting the wealth and income of the EU citizen.

The EU bank account for a citizen or a business is split into three parts. A paying in account into which salaries or wages are paid. This is the citizen's bank account number and sort code details that are used by the account holder for identification purposes. But money can only be paid into this account. If these bank details are stolen, a thief will be unable to withdraw cash from the account.

The two other accounts are debit accounts. The account holder transfers money into one debit account for the payment of standing orders and direct debits. This debit account can be used only for direct debits and standing orders and nothing else. Money is transferred to the other debit account for withdrawal of cash for ATMs by debit card and debit card purchases.

There are two important elements to this system. First, in the UK and I would assume in every other member state, every job and every sector of industry and business has a reference or identification number. When wages and salaries are paid into an account, it must be have a reference number that identifies the sector of the economy industry and job and the geographical location of the work done for which payment was made.

It will be a legal requirement of the bank to send a report, daily, weekly or monthly of the total wages paid for a job, industry sector and or geographical location to the central bank of the member state. This can then be displayed as an animated quantified flow chart on a screen. Decision makers can then see at a glance on a daily, weekly, or monthly basis the Gross Domestic Income and which sectors of the economy are increasing and which are decreasing. And since according to the discipline of Economics, Gross Domestic Income = Gross Domestic Product, the wealth that is being generated by the national economy. Also because the geographical locations of the payments are monitored, the regional distribution of wealth will be identified.

Second, there will be a facility in the system to allow a percentage of the income paid into the account to be allocated to the debit accounts, any savings accounts that the customer opens and also to the citizen's personal tax account with their countries' Inland Revenue authorities. This will reduce the cost of administering the payroll by businesses. This is a major part of the red tape that bedevils businesses. A business will have only to pay the gross wage into the employee's bank account. The percentage of the income paid would be authorized by the account holder and automatically deducted and paid into the various government tax accounts for that citizen on receipt into their account. The European Central Bank as part of the Banking System will, with the economic information forwarded by the national central banks will be able to see the relative weaknesses and strengths of the various economies. The ECB and the national central banks will be able to see on screen where the economy is getting weaker and where it is getting stronger. The decision makers can then take appropriate action because they will be able to prevent excessive busts and booms occurring in the national and international economies. The ups and downs of the economic cycle can then be kept within the limits of economic viability.

If the decision makers' policy options are televised, the option most favored by the electorate could be selected because their preferences could be displayed in the decision makers' room. This would be as close to the Greek city state democracy in Socrates' time that is possible today.

Chapter 3. The Business Components of the EU.

The Common Economic System Architecture consists of three basic types of business organization. First an Equitable limited company. In the UK, referred to as an eqPLC. Second, a Social Enterprise limited company, which I refer to in the UK as a sePLC. And thirdly, a Community Interest company, which I refer to as a ciPLC.

Of course these refer to Public Limited Companies which are legally obliged to publish audited accounts for the world to see and examine. But these types of companies which are defined by their internal work structure can be private or co-operative or common ownership companies. In the UK, I will also specify two types of sole trader self employment; public and private. Public sole traders are self employed people who will be those elected to public office and will be required to publish audited accounts of their financial affairs just as a PLC is required to do. I do not think this is essential as part of the Common Economic System Architecture of the EU. However, if the electorate believes that politicians' financial affairs need to be open to public scrutiny, then it is the country's prerogative to introduce this measure.

An equitable PLC shall have a maximum wage differential of 20 to 1. This means that the lowest paid employee in a firm is paid x monetary units per hour (Level 1) and the highest paid employee (the CEO) is paid 20x monetary units per hour (Level 20). This means that if the board of an eqPLC awards the CEO a pay rise of 100 monetary units, (per hour or per week) then the employee on the Level 1 automatically gets a pay rise of 5 monetary units, (per hour or per week).

A social enterprise company shall have a maximum wage differential of 10 to 1. The same rules will apply as to the eqPLC but the pay rates will range from Level 1 to Level 10. If the board awards a 100 monetary unit pay rise to the CEO then the Level 1 employees automatically get a 10 monetary unit pay rise.

A community interest company shall have a maximum wage differential of 5 to 1. Again the same rules apply as to the eqPLC but the pay rates will range from Level 1 to Level 5. If the board awards a 100 monetary unit pay rise to the CEO, then the Level 1 employees automatically get a 20 monetary unit pay rise.

In terms of the body politic, think of it as monitoring and enabling a viable systolic and diastolic pressure in the economy to be maintained.

The economic and sociological reasoning underlying these proposals will be stated in Part 2, the UK System in Focus.

Chapter 4. The Contract Law of the EU.

The reason for creating a new type of contract, which I believe will find favor in the EU as a whole, is based on my experience of UK contract law which is weighted against the economically weaker party to the contract. This new type of contract is called a Mutually Agreed Contract Terms (MACT) contract. The provider of the goods or service specifies what will be provided. The contractor/offeror and the contractee/offeree negotiate and agree the consideration, the money to be paid for the product or service and the length of time allowed for the payment to be made. But the purchaser of the goods or service specifies the proportion and date of the payment and/or installments to be paid.

In respect of a service that is being continuously provided such as broadband and telephone access, the monthly start and end date for which the monthly payment is made shall also be specified by the user/customer.

No penalty clauses will be allowed. Because if there is a default in the contract either by the supplier not providing the goods or service to an adequate standard or by the consumer defaulting on payment, there will be an instant remedy made by the decision of the court. The reason being decided by evidence given in a Civil Commercial court. If the supplier failed to deliver the contracted service, no money is payable to the contractor. If the consumer has defaulted on payment, the court/government pays the contractor and the consumer loses their tax allowances until the amount is paid back to the court/government. If the consumer is a PLC, the whole board of directors lose their personal tax allowances until the court/government is repaid.

This measure will support responsible businesses and business people by ensuring that cash flow is maintained. It will be visibly in a person's self interest to pay their bills on time.

Contractors will also be able to decide whether to allow credit by searching the court judgements records.

The economic and sociological reasoning for these measures are given in detail in Part 2.

Part 2. The System in Focus; The UK political economy.

The system in detail. The business components, the contractual relations between and amongst businesses, their employees and their customers are specified. Also the taxation and benefit rules are specified for individuals and firms. The purpose of these rules are to ensure that the economy is as far as possible self-regulating, thus minimizing the need for ever increasing state intervention. By establishing rules that ensure fairness for businesses and their employees and customers at source, the role of the state can be minimized as can the governments ever increasing demand for more and more taxes. By lessening the need for state intervention, there will or should be a lower demand for tax revenue. In Britain, there is a "Rip Off" culture. Indeed, there has been shown on BBC television a programme called "Rip Off Britain". For those who have not heard of the phrase "rip off" it means overcharging for goods or services that turn out be shoddy or not fit for purpose. In my opinion, this rip off culture is created by the government's ever increasing demand for more and more tax revenue which then wastes this revenue by creating more bureaucracies and red tape.

Chapter Five. The Banking System of the UK

The banking system in the UK as in the EU has at the minimum will have three accounts; a paying in (credit) account and two paying out (debit) accounts. Wages, salaries and or benefits are paid into the credit account. These payments will have an identification number that identifies the job, (in the UK the SOC number) the economic sector, and also the regional location of the recipient. This is to enable the real time monitoring of the local, regional and national economy at these levels of recursion. The total income paid to all individuals for a given job or economic sector or in a region and the percentage distribution of the different sectors of the economy will be visible to the decision makers. As time goes on, the government will be able to see which sectors of the economy are increasing or declining on a week by week or month by month basis.

Every branch of every bank will be required to send the total amount of income for each SOC number to their regional head office where these amounts are added into regional totals, These totals can be forwarded to a Bank of England "national economy monitoring unit."

The Bank Account holder will have to transfer money to the two debit accounts. The first debit account will be for standing orders and direct debits to be paid out. However, the account holder will make the decision on what date and time these payments are made with regard to the MACT contract terms that have been agreed to. For example, it can be specified that money paid into a credit account has to be made between midnight and six o'clock in the morning on the last day of the month or Friday of the week. Standing orders can be made for transfers of money from the credit account to the two debit accounts to cover the payments out on receipt of the money in the credit account. The transfers to these accounts can be specified as actual amounts or as percentages of the money received.

However, there can be other paying out accounts (as well as savings accounts which will pay a higher rate of interest than the basic rate of interest payable on the paying in account which I recommend to be set at 3% + the central bank rate). These other paying out accounts are the account holder's mortgage or rent account; and their Inland Revenue account. These accounts will pay out a percentage of the gross income that is paid into the credit account of the citizen. In a mortgage account, the amount payable will be 25% of the person's income or the actual amount of the repayment, whichever is the lower. In a rent account the amounts will be 20% of the person's income or the full rent, whichever is the lower. But of course, the mortgage holder can elect to pay 25% of their income even if that amount is greater than the repayment amount required. In the case of the rent payer, any wage earner in the property could, but not necessarily, be required to pay 20% of their income or the balance of the rent payable, whichever is the lower, even if that person is not the registered tenant.

Where these housing payments are less than the actual amount payable, the housing benefit system will make up the shortfall. This system will virtually eliminate the housing benefit bill, especially when the other benefit changes are taken into account.

The other account, the Inland Revenue payment account will receive percentage payments from the individuals credit "paying in" account. This will reduce the burden of payroll legislation on businesses. Employers would pay the employee's gross wages into their paying in credit account. Likewise, business customers would have their turnover paid into their business paying in credit account.

Mortgages and business loans. With regard to mortgages for the purchase of a person's main residential home, the maximum mortgage that will be allowed will be equivalent to a multiple, usually 3.5 times the annual income, of twenty times the legal minimum wage rate of a full time (35 hours per week) worker. The remaining amount or deposit to come out of the person's savings. Business loans would be subject to Mutually Agreed Contract Terms (MACT) contract law and penalties.

There will be no penalties for early repayment of a mortgage allowed. Also, if the bank or building society repossesses a property, the repossession will constitute the full repayment of the mortgage loan. If a property is the subject of repossession, the first refusal of taking over the property and the outstanding mortgage shall be given to the social housing association that is named by the original property buyer in the mortgage agreement.

Overdrafts.

Overdrafts will be offered to customers only on their request. The criteria to be offered an overdraft will be to have a minimum of three months income in a savings account. The overdraft will be set at 50% of three months income. The maximum overdraft that can be offered is 50% of two years income in a savings account.

The corporation tax that is payable by banks, building societies and credit card and other loan companies will be set at 10% per percentage point above 4% plus the central bank base rate. Since bank account holders are paid 3% plus the base rate interest on their credit balances and if the base rate is 0.5%, if the mortgage interest was 4.5% no corporation tax would be payable. If the mortgage interest payable was 10.5%, the corporation tax payable would be 60% of profits.

This would exert a downward pressure on the cost of mortgages and by extension the price of houses. Also, if the maximum mortgage allowed was 3.5 times the annual income of 20 times the legal minimum hourly rate of a full time (35 hours per week) employee, this would, I believe, increase the availability of funds for mortgage loans.

Appendix to Chapter 5

The identification codes for incomes will enable the total incomes for each sector of the economy to be expressed as a percentage of the total economy of the region or the nation. This can then be displayed on a screen as an animated quantified flow chart in the board rooms of district and county councils and the cabinet office. These different flow charts will display which sectors of the economy are increasing or decreasing in the different geographical areas of the country. A clever statistical analysis program (such as Cyberstride, which probably no longer exists, I assume there must be newer versions.) will be able to predict, by running the animation of the economy fast forward for five years, what is likely to happen to the economy. Also different economic policy decisions could be applied to the animation to see the effect of different policies five years hence. It would be possible to test the animated flow chart (the model of the economy) by using historical data at some point in time, and then applying the policy decisions then implemented to measure the accuracy of the model when a five year projection is made.

The reason for having separate credit accounts and debit accounts is to prevent identity theft and fraud. Debit cards would have the sort code and account number of the paying in account number only. Money can only be transferred from this account to the designated debit accounts of the account holder. Also the chip on the card would contain the jpeg portrait or the digital thumb print of the account holder. If the ATMs are fitted with a camera or a fingerprint reader, a digital photograph or thumbprint of a person making a withdrawal could be taken and compared with digital jpeg or thumb print file on the chip. If they do not match, the card would be kept within the machine and the photograph and or thumb print taken by the machine and its GPS location or address could be sent to a rapid response unit of the local police.

The reason for giving account holders the power to decide the date and time direct debits are requested is to prevent businesses attempting to take payment from an account before the income of the account holder is paid into the account. At present when a direct debit is taken from an account when there are insufficient funds available, the bank claws the money back and imposes a penalty charge on the account holder, thus causing greater impoverishment of the individual. This is immoral, unjust and unfair.

Banks make their money from making loans. These loans were and should be related to the cash deposits of its customers. Businesses create wealth and income for its owners and employees. It is only fair that a bank's customers should share in the benefits of wealth creation the bank's loans make possible. The government at present is trying to persuade banks to make loans to business. If banks are required by law to pay interest on money on deposit, they would have to provide loans in order to make a profit. Relating the amount of corporation tax payable to the net interest received by the banks and making the first 1% of net interest tax free to ensure solvency would make excessive interest payments charged by payday loan companies not feasible. A payday loan company charging 1000% interest would be liable to 10,000% corporation tax! It would be uneconomic to offer high interest loans and make a start in ending the British "rip off" culture.

The reason I stipulate mortgage loan agreements should nominate a social housing association to be offered the property in the event of repossession is to ensure continuity and stability for the family or person living in the property. However, the main clause in a mortgage agreement/contract is that repossession will constitute full repayment of mortgage. It is grossly unfair that person who loses their income for whatever reason and cannot afford to keep up the repayments to be made homeless and still be liable to pay the balance of the mortgage if the property is sold at auction at a loss. This is "putting the boot in" when a person is already down and out. I think the social housing association should take over the existing mortgage when taking possession. I call the clause that states that repossession constitutes full repayment of the mortgage the "Canary Wharf" clause.

Chapter 6. The Taxation and Legal Regulations for the Banking and Financial Sector

It will be a legal requirement for banks to pay a minimum of 3% interest on an account holder's money in a credit "paying in" account. However, it will be allowed for banks to charge £1 per week administration charge per account.

Quantitative Easing should be used to pay the 3% interest to a bank's account holders. This would at least help to stimulate demand in the economy and ease the debt burden on low income families.

Every account will have an SOC number assigned to it that will identify the job description, the economic sector and the region where the work was done. The attenuated information will be sent to the Office of National Statistics where the information will be collated and displayed as an animated flow chart showing the flow of income through the various sectors of the economy.

Taxation of banking and financial institutions shall be related to the interest charged on the loans issued. For example, banks will be charged corporation tax on the net interest charged; the amount of interest charged by the bank on loans minus the interest paid by the bank to the account holder plus the base rate. If Corporation tax is set at 10% per percentage point, the maximum net interest chargeable would be 10% making Corporation tax 100%. This would make Payday loan companies unworkable. And put a downward pressure on the cost of mortgages and business loans thus stimulating the housing market and business expansion.

With regard to credit card companies, corporation tax can be set, for example, from 2% to 5% per percentage point charged. At 5%, this would make the highest rate of interest chargeable 20% because this would create a corporation tax liability of 100%.

These tax rates would apply only to those institutions and businesses that adopted the new form of business organization. The eqPLC, the sePLC and the ciPLC.

Also, because account holders would not be allowed to have loans or overdrafts unless they have at least three months income on deposit and loans would be subject to the new Mutually Agreed Contract Terms (MACT) contract law, no penalty clauses or financial penalties would be allowed in the terms and conditions issued by the banks.

Taxation of shareholder's dividends paid by eqPLC, the sePLC and ciPLC and the equivalent private limited companies will be set at zero per cent (0%).

This can be done because the fair distribution of wealth is done at source. It was reported in the Economist in 2013 that American business men had an estimated $15 trillion kept in offshore accounts. A zero tax rate would encourage investment. Also the new MACT Contract Law that applies to the new forms of business organization ensures the cash flow of the new businesses.

Chapter 7. The Business Components of the UK

The business components of the UK include those described for the EU. The eqPLC, the sePLC and the ciPLC. The wage differentials for these different types of businesses are as specified for the EU. However the prefixes can be applied to other types of business organization that exist in the UK. For example, companies limited by guarantee, co-operatives, common ownership companies. It is the free choice of the people who form a business organization to choose which type they want to create.

However, I advocate the following regulations and rules to apply to all types of PLCs.

1. The standard full time working week is 35 hours.

2. A basic overtime rate of time and a third is paid for time worked more than the daily and weekly contracted hours. This means that if the employee's contracted hours are 16 hours per week and/or 4 hours per day, the overtime rate will be paid for hours worked for longer than these contracted hours.

3. This means that for people on a zero hours contract of employment, their pay rate would automatically have a premium of one third of that rate. However, it is my view that the only people to have no guaranteed hours of work are the self employed. So anyone on a zero hours contract should be paid a callout charge of seven hours pay.

4. The lowest rate of pay is designated as the **Level 1 pay rate.**

5. The statutory minimum wage rate is designated as the **Level 0 pay rate.** The level 0 rate is the term used for benefit payments made by the government. The level 1 pay rate paid by businesses can be the same as the level 0 hourly pay rate paid by government or higher. Level 20 is twenty times the businesses Level 1 rate. Level 020 is twenty times the Level 0 wage rate.

6. Businesses will pay a **Level 1.5 hourly rate** of 1.5 times the level 1 rate to the first line supervisors, section leader or whatever is the first rung of a promotion ladder in a business. For example, if the Level 1 rate is £7 per hour, the first rung of a promotion ladder will pay a rate of £10.50p per hour.

7. **The Bonus Pool that can be distributed amongst the Board of Directors shall not be more than the Annual wage bill of the Level 1 and the Level 1.5 employees who work a full time (35 hours) week.**

An important aspect of this system for people on these lower wage rates is the linkage between wages and benefits. Benefit entitlement will be based on the contracted weekly wage that is paid. **Not** on any overtime payments earned by the employee. A person voluntarily gives up his own time to support themselves and /or their families. **Not** the government.

Appendix to Chapter 7

These measures create system drivers that serve to create full time working weeks for more employees. The more full time employees there are, the bigger the bonuses the directors of the business can earn. "More Indians than chiefs" instead of "more chiefs than Indians" as the saying goes. Paying overtime rates for hours worked over seven hours per day and thirty five hours per week will ensure that managers and accountants work out the optimum number of employees in the new form of business. Directors could not give themselves an "ivory tower" pay rise without regard to their employee base and their wage rate. Directors will need to look at the total wage bill of the company when deciding pay rates. Zero hours contracted employees would have to be paid overtime rates for any hours they worked.

Paying 1.5 times the level 1 rate would incentivize people to try for promotion and become more involved with the success of the business.

The total bonus pool and the profits made by a business must be made public knowledge in the company accounts. The shareholders will have the right to decide or recommend at the company AGM, what proportion of the profits will be distributed as dividends.

However, I believe the primary effect of these measures is the culture change (culture shock) from a rip off, bullying bureaucratic system of the market economy to a respectful social economy.

Chapter Eight. The Taxation Regulations for the Utilities and Business Components.

This is the first time that the term "Utilities" has been used in this book. The reason is that the Utility companies are, like the financial institutions, are essential to the working of a modern society. The utility business components include those businesses that provide water and sewerage services, electricity and gas. The demands for these services are relatively inelastic in economic terms. Consequently, their customers can be held to ransom in terms of having price rises foisted upon them regardless of the market conditions in which the companies operate. Therefore there should be special rules of taxation and the types of business component that are allowed to provide these services.

First, a utility company must be either an sePLC or a ciPLC. Since corporation tax is based on the maximum wage differential allowed by the type of business component, an sePLC with a wage differential allowed of 10 to 1 would pay a corporation tax rate of 10% on profits, a ciPLC would pay a corporation tax rate of 5%. However, the maximum profit a utility company can make must be related to the total annual wage bill of the level 1 employees. Any profits that are made above the annual wage bill must be refunded to its customers in proportion to their consumption. Alternatively, especially in the case of the energy companies, a standing charge could be calculated based on the minimum energy consumption

In this way, energy costs can be minimized and budgeted for by consumers. Profligate energy consumption above a standard amount could be charged at a slightly higher rate.

TAXATION OF SHAREHOLDER'S DIVIDENDS OF THE NEW BUSINESS COMPONENTS SHALL BE ZERO.

The reason for this that the fair distribution of wealth is done at source. Consequently, a complicated redistributive tax system is not required.

Governments do not have the money, nor is it their purpose, to invest in new businesses. Private investors do; but like anyone else, they do not like to be ripped off by avaricious governments. Likewise, employees do not like being ripped off by avaricious businesses and governments.

Taxation of the new business components will be subject to corporation tax and earned income relief; a "personal earned income tax relief" for businesses. A business will be able to earn annual profits equal to the annual wage bill of the level1 and level1.5 employees before it becomes liable to pay corporation tax.

As said before, the percentage corporation tax rate is related to the type of business component. An eqPLC, 20%; sePLC, 10% and a ciPLC 5%.

Making shareholders dividends zero tax rated will increase the value of pension funds and make the UK and the EU a tax haven. Temporarily at least.

It is assumed that the purpose of business is to provide goods and services in order to make a profit, i.e., the economic self interest of the managers and shareholders. It is also in the economic self interest of the System 1 employees (re the Viable System Model) to be well paid enough to have a disposable income.

In Systems Thinking terms, another causal loop to make this possible is to relate the rate of Corporation tax to the ACTUAL wage differential implemented by the business. An eqPLC that has a statutory wage differential of 20 to 1 has a Corporation tax rate of 20%. However, if the actual wage differential implemented by the eqPLC is 8 to 1, then the Corporation tax rate would be 8%. Less than the statutory wage differential of an se PLC.

A mathematical exercise for national treasuries and international firms of accountants.

Create a graph with the hourly rates of all employees from the CEO to the lowest hourly rate of the System 1 employees along the x axis and the number of employees on each hourly rate on the y axis. If my understanding of mathematics is correct (I am not a mathematician), the area under the curve is the total wage bill.

Now, keeping the area under the curve the same (or even z% less) create a graph with a wage differential of 20 to 1 or less and calculate the optimum wage differential and the number of full-time 35 hour week employees that would maximise profits.

For the think tanks and economists, how much more demand would be generated in the economy if income inequality was reduced in this way?

Chapter Nine. The Benefit System of the UK.

Currently, the benefit system of the UK creates poverty, depression, alcoholism, obesity drug addiction. The basic operation of the current system creates frustration, stress and depression. The health issues listed above are the coping mechanisms people use to deal with these stresses. The hopelessness the system engenders creates the vicious circle of benefit dependency. The changes proposed here can only be done if the Banking System is changed as advocated earlier.

First, new parents, either the mother or the father, will, subject to acquiring an NVQ (National Vocational Qualification) in parenting skills, be entitled to a Parenthood Allowance which will be set at the minimum wage rate times 100 hours. At the time of writing, the minimum wage rate is £6.19p so the Parenthood Allowance would be £619 per week. Since housing benefit is based on paying the balance of rent due after the bank has allocated 20% of the tenant's income or the full rent, whichever is the lower, to the landlord and Social Housing rents are around the £100 per week level, this would virtually eliminate the Housing Benefit bill. Twenty percent of £619 is £123.80p.

Child benefit would be replaced by the Parenthood Allowance. People already in receipt of Child Benefit will be able to continue to receive it unless they choose to earn the NVQ in Parenting Skills. New parents will not have that choice. However, a grandparent of the new child will also be eligible if they have legal care and control of the child and acquire the NVQ.

1. The reasoning behind these proposals is that every family will have a qualified child carer. A super nanny in every family!
2. This will create an oversupply of child care provision. Thereby reducing the cost of childcare.
3. It will create equality between men and women in the workplace. Either sex may suspend their career progression to start and care for their family. Therefore;
4. Men and women will both have to face the same "glass ceiling" to promotion.

Job Seekers Allowance will be replaced by a Personal Development Allowance. This will be set at the minimum wage rate times fifteen hours. Three hours a day for five days a week. £6.19p times 15 hours equals £92.85p per week. To qualify for this benefit a person must not be in work or be in receipt of Parenthood Allowance.

They must be on a further education course in a GCSE of their choice to qualify for the benefit. However, a person will still qualify for the benefit for 12 weeks after starting employment. The employer will not have to pay wages for the first eight weeks of the claimant's employment. However, the employer will be required to provide the relevant NVQ training that is necessary for their employment. If the employee does not reach the standard the employer requires, termination of employment would occur. It will be up to the employer to make the job an attractive proposition for the employee. Neither the employer nor the employee will be penalized by the government for trying out new opportunities.

People who are made redundant will be immediately entitled to government funded re-training in the foundation course of a new career change.

Another qualification for the Allowance is to do fifteen hours of voluntary work per week that is documented by the voluntary organization. The claimant's fifteen hours of activity can be split between education and voluntary work.

The important point is that a benefit must be earned. There can be no such thing as a free lunch.

An alternative name for this benefit is the Personal Development and Community Involvement Allowance.

Sickness Benefit. The following rules apply only to employees of the new type of business organization described in this book. The first six weeks off work through illness will be funded out of the employee's savings. This will reduce capricious absenteeism. From six weeks to six months off work due to incapacity the full wage of the employee will be paid by the employer. Six months and more, the incapacitated individual will be supported by the government.

In this chapter we have been looking at the individual instead of an organization of a business. However, there are individuals who are self employed or a sole trader or a sub contractor. So it seems appropriate to look at the tax regime tradesmen and entrepreneurs could be subject to.

The taxation and benefit system should have as its design output the self reliance and increased self esteem of the individuals who are subject to it.

The personal tax relief should apply to individuals only. Whether a person is in a relationship or not is no business of the state. Taxation and benefit rules should apply to individuals only regardless whether a person is married, cohabiting or house sharing.

Tax relief should be re-named Community Involvement Allowance. To qualify for this tax allowance, a person must be a member of their local Resident's Association. The Resident's Association must be registered with the local parish or district council. A person who is "offshore" for tax purposes will not qualify for tax relief; they would have to pay tax on the whole of their income.

Tax relief for self–employed people would enable them to earn 100 times the minimum wage rate (£619 per week currently) before being liable for income tax. The tax liability of a sole trader whose turnover was paid into the new type of banking system could be calculated automatically and paid into the government's Inland Revenue account.

However, I propose a new type of self employment. This is the Public Sole Trader. A Public Sole Trader is a person who has been democratically elected to Public Office and receives an income from the Public Purse (taxation). The main requirement of this type of self-employment will be to publish annual audited accounts.

Chapter Ten. The Contract Law of the UK.

The new type of contract law is the Mutually Agreed Contract Terms (MACT) law.

This law will apply only to the new types of business organization that specify the wage differential between the highest and lowest paid employees. The maximum being 20 to 1.

The important part of this new type of contract is that the customer/client/consumer of the goods or services provided specifies the time and date the consideration due leaves their account. This is because a person has no control when a payment is received by the provider of the goods or services. If a contractor needs a payment to cover a delay, then an advance stage payment can be negotiated.

The second proviso is that MACT contracts will not have any penalty clauses imposed by either party to the agreement. This is because the contract will be enforced by new penalties imposed in law in a new type of commercial court.

Here are two examples;

A) A newsagent provides a newspaper delivery service. A customer defaults on his monthly paper bill. It will be assumed that the newsagent stops delivery within two weeks of default.

B) A sub contractor provides precision engineering components to a global PLC. The PLC delays payment longer than the usual thirty days.

In both cases, the court is notified automatically of the delay in the payment of monies due. If the court finds in favor of provider of the goods or service, the court pays the money due to the provider and the personal Community Involvement tax allowance is removed from A) the newsagent's customer or B) the Board of Directors of the global PLC until the money and the court costs have been reimbursed to the court.

Regarding mortgage contracts and agreements, the minimum mortgage allowed will three time the annual income of a 35 hour working week on a Level 0 wage. The maximum mortgage allowed on a main residential property will be three times the annual income of a 35 hour working week on a Level 020 wage. These criteria will apply to the main residential property of the mortgage holder. Repossession of the property by the mortgagor shall constitute full repayment of the mortgage. The Canary Wharf clause.

Also the property must be offered to a Social Housing Association for the amount of mortgage outstanding with the current householder as a sitting tenant. It will be possible for the mortgage provider to require a mortgage repayment of 25% of the total household income, at least for the first five years of the mortgage. However, the mortgage holder will be able to pay more than the actual repayment due without being liable to any penalty whatsoever for early repayment of the mortgage.

Appendix. The Purpose and Problems of the Common Economic System Architecture.

The purpose of this design for Freedom and Fairness in the economy is precisely that. To produce and maximize personal freedom (but not licence) and to ensure fairness (economic justice). This design is an economic regulatory system that needs to be enacted in its entirety as a complete operating system. It is not feasible to take bits here and bits there. It wont work for the same reason the current system does not work and is not fit for purpose. Like Johnny Cash's car it was built "one piece at a time".

Paying a Parenthood Allowance to a family may well reduce ADD because a parent can afford to be at home to pay full attention to their child. A Dr. Gabor Matte of Canada says ADD and ADHD are caused by stressed parenting. If this is true, one of the stresses of family life will be much reduced; lack of money. Paying a Parenthood Allowance will, in combination with the other changes, eliminate the Housing Benefit bill for government, reduce the special needs burden on schools, create equality of opportunity between men and women in the workplace and reduce the demand for employment thus putting upward pressure on wages.

By giving business organizations an earned income/profits allowance based on the wage bill of full time Level 1 and Level 1.5 employees. and a reduced wage bill because of the limitation of the wage differentials to 20 to 1, this will increase the number of full time jobs that will be created. This will reduce the number of benefit claimants and/or the amount of benefit claimed.

The new banking system will reduce the burden of bureaucracy and red tape on businesses because the businesses will be able to pay the gross wages into their employee's bank accounts with their current SOC number. The tax due will be paid out of the employee's account into his Inland Revenue account.

In the event of the tax credit system continuing, the benefit payable must be related solely to the contracted weekly rate paid. Overtime monies earned must be exempted from the benefit calculation. Extra hard work must not be penalized by the government.

By allowing businesses to take on employees without having to pay wages for the first eight weeks of employment and requiring to train them to acquire the relevant NVQ, employers can "road test" employees before offering a permanent contract. And because employment will not result in loss of benefit, claimants will not have the stress of being without an income if they have re-apply for benefit if the employment turns out not to be suitable either for the employer or the employee.

There are design problems to be resolved with the new system. The system creates linkages between the people who decide the wage rates, those on the Level 20 rate and those who do not have that power. Who does the algedonic monitoring to ensure that the differentials are not exceeded? This could be the banks. It could be that the wages paid into a person's account must state the Level number, hourly rate and the total wage paid. It could be an internal System Three management function or a trade union function, which could be internal to the company or external to it. In any case, the auditors of the company accounts will be charged with ensuring that there is compliance with differentials. However, the point of a viable system is that algedonic monitoring occurs in real time as the wages and salaries are paid.

Who should support the introduction of the new system?

The "government" should support it because it goes a long way to solving the pension crisis.

Liberal Democrats should support the system because it would create a level playing field across the whole of the EU and produce economic and social well-being in the country.

Conservatives should support it because it ensures "responsible capitalism"

Socialists and trade unionists should support it because it prevents "rip off" capitalism and government.

The CBI should support it because it reduces red tape and bureaucracy.

The Federation of Small Businesses should support it because it allows people to earn a living wage and reduces the accounting burden on traders.

Global capitalists, investors and fund managers should support the system because no taxation will be payable on dividend income and the cash flow will be ensured by the new MACT contract law system.

The European Parliament should enact the legislation necessary because it will open the door to international global investors in the struggling economies.

The people as a whole should support the system because it will increase their disposable income.

This book describes **what** needs to be done. It does not show **how** the continuous monitoring of the economy is done.

In VSM terminology, who carries out the System 3 and System 3* function. I call upon the academic and scientific communities to resolve these issues.

Acknowledgements.

https://www.youtube.com/watch?v=G0R09YzyuCI This is a video by Joseph Tainter of Utah University about the collapse of civilizations. What I found of interest was his phrase that "organizations channel human behavior". I believe that the organizations described in this book will channel behaviors that will make society and the economy sustainable, more cohesive and free.

Professor Russell Ackoff also explains in a YouTube/Tedtalk why and how systems work.

Javier Livas has uploaded an interesting YouTube video titled "Super Cybernetics". This video explains the history, development and the range of applications of the science of cybernetics amongst the various fields and disciplines of scientific enquiry.

Raul Espejo in his website "Syncho" gives a critique of the EU in terms of a scientific and cybernetic analysis.

Printed in Great Britain
by Amazon.co.uk, Ltd.,
Marston Gate.